M000218825

A DOOR ON THE RIVER

A DOOR ON THE RIVER

poems

Jessica Hornik

CHATWIN BOOKS

SEATTLE

Poems copyright the author, 1992–2018

ISBN 978-1-63398-063-1
Trade Paperback

ISBN 978-1-63398-059-4
Limited Signed Hardcover Edition

Edited by Phil Bevis. Editorial and design content copyright
Chatwin Books, 2018. All rights reserved.
Cover design by Annie Brulé.
Cover image by Oleksandra Fedorova via Shutterstock.
Author photo by Rex Wilder.

Visit us on the web at www.ChatwinBooks.com

for Mark, my beloved

for Zachary and Ethan

and for Rex Wilder
"Friendship how rare!"

Table of Contents

IV. Stars or Other Distances

Acknowledgments

I. A Blue Like No Other

August

Sighing as I go,
exhaling summer's heat—
I'm done. Done
introducing the goldenrod
to the roadside society
of asters. My final act.
September wakes now
to a blue like no other,
a glazed transparency,
the sunlight downright
urgent on the backs
of blackbirds. The river
sparkles hard, as though
an unglimpsed immortality
pressed up from below.
As though.

A Hundred Skies

A hundred skies passed in a day; the one
world was bare. The trees, asterisks
marking the places your eye wandered
along the bottom of the sky, resisted
the wind's urge to pinwheel them westward.
The meadow, dry and beige as a beach,
for weeks had likened itself to a
strangely tinted snow, and so was ready.
It seemed if you were to follow the road
off the edge of the scene, you might alight
in a forbidden springtime, whose absolute
negative these acres had to be. And yet
you would not about-face, abandon this
about-to-be, you whose forehead
was a mountain bluff marked for first snows,
so cold had it been for days behind your eyes.
Ah, winter! Stalled like Orion on the horizon,
foot caught on a hook of mountain,
eyeing the rise of the cold plate of moon.

Song for Five O'Clock

Take your chair and follow the sun
until the afternoon light is done
stirring the mayflies above your hair
and chiding the moss for treading the stair.
The garden's in ruins but the pool
is kept full. Sinister fiddlehead ferns unspool
in the field across the road.
The hills buckle under their load
like camels coming to their knees.
You feel a sadness you can't appease
when the squirrels bicker in the upper
branches—soon you'll go in for supper.
Then clouds will mime the onset of the night,
and birds forget their lines of flight.

Cold Comfort

Roadside weeds have the saddest
autobiographies. From brown to brown,
their seasons are only an idea.
I collect branches of early juneberry,
whose fate was sealed by late sleet.
Indoors, grateful for a glass
of lukewarm water, they join me
for an open-minded morning. This being open,
though, sooner or later, makes us both weep.

For the hills, populated by a hardy tribe
of northern trees, have piled my intentions
up into the clouds. The meadow's soft
edges were prearranged, amenable to feeding deer,
while I go on bumping into furniture,
and roll around on castered chairs,
accumulating cups of one inch of cold coffee.
The clouds are splitting hairs. Bruises
turn green faster than this spring.

A landscape abandoned by its painter
is propped against my wall.
I appreciate the camaraderie of a cast-off,
with its overwrought road slashing
through green fields. Things too well made
can get on one's nerves. Imagine the fingerprint
of a thought: a pattern of sunlight
crashing through an opened door, retreating
with the slam. It was true. And unrepeatable.

Pleasant Bay

Because it rained all day, everyone grew sad.
Those already sad grew sadder.
The cupped blossoms of the wild strawberries
broadcast through the fields
drained as quickly as they filled,
while we were filled up
and kept on filling, like clocks ticking
after the end of the world.

Second Day on Garnet Lake

Had yesterday's water lilies not closed
their blossoms by midmorning, I might not
have lured you so early from bed, clothing you
kiss by kiss, promising an afternoon
of hours left to their own devices.
So short a white spell on the blue of the bay—
we had to act. The canoe parted the lily pads
as your hand sometimes knows
the way my hair should go. I grabbed onto a sturdy,
all-yellow lily as we passed; its rubbery stem
came up out of the water only far enough
to reproach me. It held fast to its
prize, its portion set aside for the world.
I was reminded of the time when, in a museum,
I approached the back of a statue, and touched
the lifelike spine—alarms were ringing, ringing.
The lily pads went under
as the canoe went over, and rose in our wake.

Third Day on Garnet Lake

The trees on the lake bottom have fallen into
rocklike sleep. Their bark has gone to elephant skin.
From some, branches poke skyward, a forest
for perch. Heart-shaped leaves broach
the surface—whether weeds attached
to a defenseless host, or the tree's own
pangs of former glory, I suppose only lake dwellers
could tell you. One told us how the southern land
had been purposely flooded
to form this expanse hardly deeper
than an oar's length. Canoe through the deeps past
the stubbly shelf of grass and you find yourself
atop a thicket too available to the eye for comfort.
Only some of the trees guide you
by showing their roots in the air. The water
you glide through is a burial ground
not meant to be visited by your respect.
You would not want to be present if the trees
regained their element—
should the northern dam be broken
and they let the water go.

Part of a Lifetime

On this day in October
I was driving over the train tracks
and ahead of me saw
what looked like a big black puddle
in the middle of the pavement.
Then the mass of starlings trembled
and from its center rose up, pulling
its edges along with it,
as though an invisible magnet
had been lowered over a saucer
of iron shavings. By the time my car passed,
starling regiments chattered at ease
on the crisscrossed power lines.
I wonder what's worse, transitions
or the lack of them.
The trees along the edge of the field
waved their fauvist flags, but not
at me, not at any of us.

The White Pines

"After great pain, a formal feeling comes–"
—Emily Dickinson

They brought home
the six-inch white pine seedlings in the trunk
of the white Impala with the ruby-red upholstery.
My father's project was to change
a quarter-acre of our yard into a private forest.
With my mother he staked out the rows. The soil
was easy, nothing like the rocky clay I fight with
to win the rights to my daisies and daylilies,
though my yard is just the next town over
from the one in the past. I watched
the planting, I don't know for how long.
You see the end of this story
coming from miles away: the monumental
white pines, me driving past them one day
with my children, now old enough for me to say,
look, my father planted those a long time ago,
at the stop sign showing them with my hands
the height of six inches, their moment
of silent amazement—more, I think,
at the evidence of this father
missing from the action of our lives
than at the manmade forest itself.

Calamity Jane,
someone once called my mother.
A compound fracture on the slick patio flagstones
two weeks before my wedding didn't stop her
from walking me down the aisle on crutches,
wearing one lilac shoe to match her lilac dress.
It's not enough to have cancer, she joked,
I have to have a broken leg too.

I envy those
who feel watched over. On the other hand,
after my mother died the small transgressions
became easy—buying a microwave,
ordering with abandon from a catalogue, neglecting
to sew on buttons—the seal of disapproval
having been removed. No longer a daughter,
I performed my daughterly duties:
took care of the estate, thanked her friends,
resolved that, over time, I would teach
my children who she was, knowing
my older son's memory of his two years with her
would shake clean like an Etch-a-Sketch.
Some nights I still think of my unintended
transgression—that I sold her sewing box,
with its lifetime collection of odds and ends,
along with the unwanted dishes and furniture.
The formal feeling not yet come.

Like my kindergarten child,
I'm learning to count by fives and tens.
Friends I've known for twenty years.
Places I haven't been for twenty-five years.
Summer memories that level me with their intensity
after thirty years. And so on. The last house
my parents rented at Paradox Lake
the cat adapted to like a prince to the summer palace.
Roaming the pine forests, he brought mice home
to us alive, which my mother then shooed with a broom
across the faded linoleum and out
the screen door. And out the screen door
the cat would chase again and our Scrabble game
resume. My memory slips out after him,
hurrying to hunt for the untold stories
scattered through time
that make up one consciousness
before the door slams behind.

The Less I See

1.

The leaves are down. The lines of the western hills
now connect. *A* and *I* of roof and chimney rise legibly
on branches' blank lines. In the mornings we lie together
in the palm of the bed, then observe the kitchen rituals,
kiss goodbye at the back door. The house becomes
the vast deserted station of my thoughts, whose arrivals
and departures the second hand chases down their tracks.
I grow invisible between words I have already used
and those that await their sentence.

2.

Three Norway spruces
drape across the roof
of the house opposite
like the sleeves of women
gesturing across a table.
The sun disappears, trailing
its colors to no purpose
but that time might
see itself passing
in the eyes of space.

3.

In the evenings, when I wait for you, disappointment
has taught me the languages of all our neighbors' cars.
But the countries of their houses remain closed
to exploration or trade. In the provinces of bedrooms and dens
laws are made and broken. Lawns are mown
down like invading armies. The eye scouts the lamp-lit windows
for signs of interior motives. And in the empty halves
of double lots, where wilderness supplants
the carefully chosen adjoining plants, not just another language
is necessary, but one wholly submissive to the sourceless
messages that crowd the earth, words without alphabets.

4.

In the kitchen, pitched like a sultan's tent
spilling light and music in the middle of a desert,
we shepherd the day to its close. My own voice
comes to me like a shadow without shape; yours, like the secret
missing counterpart of my ear. To anyone
who might ask, I could explain marriage:
I move into you, as into a dream house, and never leave.

To R., on His Ocean Adventure

The sea is all odds
and no even. Mid-Atlantic,
there's no break
in the action.
But on the page in your lap,
caesuras and stanzas
break salty and deep.
Words swim in the cold
friendless void, oddly
finned. In a nightmare
a sailor scoops up
your wife and vanishes.
Remember when land's end
seemed spectacular,
romantic, extreme?
Out there only your bed
has the quality of land,
a parking lot
for jangled joints.
The waves' popcorn
overflows. And the freighter,
a floating nation,
seems an inversion
of expansion. It sails
beneath the flag
of your green eyes.
The books you brought
are useless: written
in a land language,
they cannot sing the sea's
high C's. In a few days
Antwerp will warp
from the horizon, a rip

in this newfangled
cosmic seam. When you take
your first step on shore,
dear friend,
do a riff on Lot's wife:
in this variation,
your last look back
renders you not a pillar
but the embodiment
of a wave, endlessly
gathering, cresting.

Charms Against Fall

Rain
From the upstairs bedroom rain is the fog of dreams still lifting.
A motorboat idling
off Assembly Point strikes a pitch your last dream cannot recover.
The sheet of metal
lying at the cabin's feet is splattered into being.
Beside it a fern
admits rain without checking for tickets. And you accept him,
a man lacking credentials
in pain. The roof is the final stop of falling: you lie at the end
of a certain world.

Mist
At the next house a second world begins
in a ride to Cleverdale for supplies. Brake lights
like red columbine stenciled on the mist.
Along the porch a row of marigolds you feel sorry for—
middle sisters outshone by daylilies and black-eyed Susans.
Today rain will keep you indoors where the world's voices fail.

Cedar
Open the cedar chest where the quilts are stored—
swoon in the wood's breath, a tree's open tomb.
Hear the thud of the dock moored
in camelback waves. Maple leaves bleed
the summer out of you. The weather will never be right.

Clouds
The mailbox is forlorn, like a woman
awaiting her missing-in-action.
There are dishes to wash but you can't remember
what you have eaten, if you have eaten.
The hours, like the bags of bottles
left under the sink, wait to be redeemed.
This morning a gentle voice

woke you piece by piece:
Admit that clouds are good at least
for warding off the shadows' sure advance,
and rain is kinder on the face
than sun. Yes, but summer billowed like harem pants
and today is the cinch at the waist.

Waves
Naked before you,
I hold this page.
Ah, the look in your eyes
as I left our bed!
From where I woke
folds of linen foam
against your back.
Waves break—
first crest, then lack.

At Steepletop

I.

This is the morning of the flowering quince.
Up from the stone pool, where pine needles lie
like shorn red hair around the twig chairs,
the garden resumes its pilgrim's progress.
If we thought jonquils were its pinnacle,
behold the blushing quince. Scentless,
it revels in a scent unknown to us.
Its cupped blossoms mark places in the air
we can't turn back to.

2.

Let this place anchor in memory
like the birdless birdbath sunk into pine needles.
Let its aspect take on the colors of marble benches
sitting sixty-five years in sun and rain:
blue, rose, gold, shadow, pearl.
These pines first schooled the wind in speech.
These fiddlehead ferns, scrolled
threats in the meadow,
I love as I love my nightmares—
the clearest idea of terror,
against which all calm is measured.

3.

Calm, calm, the slats of the blue-green bench
break in waves of shadow on the stone wall.
The sound of the stream is everywhere.
Marsh marigolds blossom by it
like water bursting into another dimension—
the stare of sound. And the shadblow,
coeval with the hatching of the shad,
flicks its white petals like ash.

4.
The sky was everything it wanted to be.
The clouds were stiff asters
snapped from their stems. And the moon
fairly trembled among them, as a man overcome
by too-great joy shakes his head,
softly, a no saying yes.

5.
I was dreaming of you
while you were dreaming of me.
We were two characters on facing pages
in a book closed by night.

The Statue of Zeus

Every October, the giant maple
in front of Deb and Charlie's house
was the wonder of the neighborhood.
Until this fall, when I braced myself
as their yard filled up with trucks.
Before long, blue sky and sunlight
swept out the radiant red,
and the tree was a shadow
of nothing, a stump to be ground down
another day. I thought of the page
in the boys' book of ancient wonders
showing Phidias' statue of Zeus,
which towered for centuries
at Olympia, then disappeared
to where only time can look at it.
My gaze stumbles over the spot now
as it travels clear out to the field.

Now I See It

The world spread wide outside my window
is a dictionary, for every time I look up
I learn something. This morning the subject
was mist. I studied its forms: the thickness
of its noun, fresh from the mountain,
its adjectives murmuring in the grass, then
the verb of its vanishing. Next,
the soft declensions of the whistling swans,
looked up under *V. A* is for apple tree
empty of apples, whose falling occasioned
the round red Absolute's ascent into air.
And in the meadow—fleeting as a definition
a thousand times consulted and as many times
forgot (O Robin-Hood mind that thieves
to give, itself forever rich and forever poor)—
the deer, bounding soundlessly
into the speckled edge of woods.

Raving Beauty

I.

The Unrequited Lover's Lament

You were pure corona
some days—I was allowed
a glimpse—and some days
you were full-on darkness.
Some days it was best
to look away.
You gave me little else
but my own shadow,
and so I shadowed you.
I sang for you.
I was the vowel slipped in
among your consonants.
I was your constant.
I never suffered and I suffered
always—me, me
with my sun-burnt heart.

2.

The Sisters

Autumn escalates
through the maples
at the edge of the park
and poses gloriously

on the brink.
Summer scowls, oh so
monochromatically green
with envy. But one windy day

is the end of it—
think of Wharton
at work in her
Lenox bed, tossing

page after page
to the floor.
The sisters exit
and winter

enters the marbled
room, all gray
glamour, blood
relative of no one.

3.
Rushing Through the Garden

Rushing through the garden,
I almost stop near the sprays
of budding coralbells,

each stalk dotted
with tiny, compact globes.
You let go of my hand

to approach the mass of irises,
floating like Cleopatra's barge
in a becalmed world.

Around us stone walls
are going back to the earth.
The one iris you decide

no one will miss,
its golden-furred center
an explorable wilderness,

has a future in a glass of water.
Look at those, I say, turning
toward a regiment of peonies.

But you know what you like.
You know where we've been.

II. The Invisible Woman

The Invisible Woman

In the hospital for the terminally unseen,
she resorted to screaming,
but the sense of the things she screamed
got lost—the voice being
an unreliable narrator of the scene
of the mind. Though she had committed
herself, she had been driven
to her condition by others:

The father, who had died before she was even
seventeen, left her to imagine
the earth as the thing separating
the dead from the living,
a curtain so much denser and darker
than darkness. "The dead don't see
us, and we see them only in dreams,"
was one of the things she screamed.

Friends, neighbors, acquaintances—
they saw nothing at all
unusual in her, nothing, certainly,
to which the term "eccentric" could be applied.
Moving among them as one of them,
she wondered if love of one's fellows
was, in fact, an insidious form of self-betrayal.
And all the sundry people
she spent her life's days with—tellers
at the drive-thru, supermarket cashiers,
UPS men, mechanics . . . oh, the conspiracy was grand
to turn her into what she seemed!
"Though not of my choosing,
invisibility is my grand theme,"
was one of the things she screamed.

What about the husband?
Like two flashlights whose beams

are shined into each other
head-on with the faces touching,
the intensity of their twinned brightness
left but a faint rim of light,
like an echo, for the world to see.
Her love for him, and his for her, was, then,
another thing about her that went unseen.

And the baby? He saw his mother.
That was what she was,
as far as his eyes could see.
That at the age of, say, twenty-three
he would not remember the love
she had lavished on his one-year-old self
drove her to an absurd despair.
His future could not behold
her present. And yet, when she peered down
the river of his being, she saw no choice
but to pour herself in.
"If I loved him to any greater extreme,
I would disappear,"
was one of the things she screamed.

She tried to laugh at herself
and her ridiculous need:
to free the soul from its private quarters
of personality, to let its within and without
be the same thing—like a water lily
yoking above and below to a single beauty.
In the hospital for the terminally unseen,
she settled in like a deep-sea creature
on the floor of a vastness, accustomed
to the pressure and its attendant lack of light.

The Invisible Woman Continued

She paced her house like a guard in a museum—
but here, telephone, stove, high chair, china closet, Tonka truck
were no one's last work or recovered masterpiece or attempt at post-
modernity. Her children were not performance artists.
Their tantrums and ecstasies won no grants
but her begrudged attention, were as real as—
but then, she was too much a child of her times
to complete the analogy.

There was a gap between the things she thought of
and the things she'd actually do—a waiting room she sanely
backed out of. She didn't take her son's crayons
and write on the living-room wall whatever it was she believed
no one understood about her, or lie down on the floor
and stay there, immobile for hours. It was, after all was said
and done, impossible to obtain the solemn promise
that someone would see her now.

She had tried to impose a deficit-reduction plan—
hiring babysitters, trading off weekend duty with her husband—
but the effort to replenish energy, meaning, silence
and solitude, former cornerstones of a decently lived day,
had restored her not to balance but to a perilous
zero: a blank so filled in it was still blank.
It was no great leap from exhaustion of this magnitude
(a word not carelessly chosen, for she felt as though she fairly

shone in her endurance) to thoughts of the nearest bridge.
Such thoughts were, of course, merely little enticing exit ramps
when mind and limbs slowed to a snail-like procession carried out
for form's, for necessity's, for appearance's sake. She waved
tiny rhythmic waves to the onlookers safely beyond
the cordon sanitaire of her suffering, her shoulders,
still proud as in the early stages of her youth, emblazoned
with her own stock reply to her own self-pity: *other people*

have it so much worse. Still, was thirty-three too old
to be an orphan? She glanced at her parents (in the famous
rowboat snapshot), who, by not returning the gesture,
effaced her, as though she were the mirror of their evanescence.
It was better to look out the window. Across the street
she saw the afterimages of the two towering pines

cut down last spring for a family room and garage,
and the two pines formerly hidden by the two departed.
See, her mother had said then, ever one to console, you can still see
two trees—two minus two is still two. No, she said to herself now,
I don't see—can absence rhyme with presence? With the dwindling
wealth of her memory, she tried to buy the sight unseen.

Sightseeing with the Invisible Woman

This winter the cat had nothing to do but inventory
the comfort levels of various items of furniture, installing
a democracy of fleas throughout the house. This winter

the birdfeeder went largely unvisited, and eyes
went hungry. This winter boxes of newly inherited
    family documents,
portraits, bundles of letters, all aging well past the death dates

of their subjects and authors, were left to fend for themselves
in the uninsulated space she gave them. This winter
inwardness yielded a screen: she saw within

the same snowfields the family saw on Sunday drives
    through country
made virgin again, the immaculate misconception snow visits
on vistas. On such excursions, as the four-year-old
    announced sightings

of every animal, vehicle, and natural wonder, she imagined herself
a witness to his mind's formation, his mind a receiver
that had by now begun transmitting images

to the future of his memory. Someday these random moments
would come back to him, and somehow she would be there,
an interpreter, however implicit, of his past. (The present,

her present, was like a photograph whose area matched
her field of vision, with her parents, right and left, standing
just outside the frame.) This winter she took the baby
    each morning

to look out his window at the silver maple, which rose up to them
like an arrested fountain. She hoped he would learn to love,
intricately, the world, as though it were a face

turned benignantly toward him. This winter counted five divorces
and one wedding, while she tried to decide if the seven years
of her own married life seemed like a long or a short time,

and was shaken by the delicacy of its very strength. This winter
she drank as much coffee as she pleased, and took forever
to finish reading the paper, and after her husband left for work

she and the boys went about their business
like a union in the light industry of everyday life.
Now and then, when looking out through the layered lace

of curtain and snow at a world turned black and white
as a soccer ball, she was held there—as if by a pressure:
her children behind her, their blind faith in the rightness

of her every move, the enormous normalcy she adhered to
for their sakes, and hence her own. Granted,
she often had the sense of hibernating with insomnia.

But she was thankful for the formal esthetics of pine trees
        under fresh snow,
and for the little northern lake they passed one
        post-storm afternoon
that brought *peace* to mind as a fine off-rhyme for *ice*.

The Invisible Woman Surfaces

I.

Now that the baby has gone to bed,
I'm carving a solitude
out of the tree of sleep
he's perched in. With husband
and older child happily
packed off, I tour my thoughts
like a cache of long-lost paintings
finally on view.

2.

Drought-stricken petunias drip over the sides
of the window boxes. My hand, which ought to lift
the watering can from its nail, subsides like a tide
on the chair's arm. Does stillness, with its reputation
for depth, or substance, have me anchored here,
or merely idling before the next required move?
I feel as though every coming moment
has me in its clutches.

3.

Lake water trembles down from the north.
The marble clock lords on the mantel
like a king come out on his balcony
to view his subjects. There is something
I ought to be doing, a duty
I should be fulfilling. Tyrannical
summer afternoons, the sun handing out invitations
impossible to refuse—won't it ever rain?

4.

And here we find a portrait
of the self, seasonless rose
rooted below the surface

of light and time.
From this hillside over the lake
light is synonymous with change
as it rides the self-canceling waves.

5.
Later, scores of gulls begin to settle on the water
as though parts of one organism controlled
by a central command. Over and over
I watch for the last wingbeat between flying
and floating, after which each wave
becomes a gull's camouflage, a test
for the naked eye's powers of observation.

6.
I take the baby monitor with me
to the water's edge and sit down on the dock.
I check my watch—no time for a swim—
then dip my hand in the water, my hand
a variation on a gull diving down
for food, and pull it back shining
from its foray into another element. I look up
at the far mountains surrounding the lake:
the earth's heartbeats traced on a chart of sky.

The Invisible Woman at Her Mirror

1.

In college, in the apartment on Highland Place,
she sometimes viewed herself as though perched
near the bedroom ceiling. There she was
down below, in various stages
of distress or elation, engaged in sex or solitude.
It was the self doubled, or the self fractured,
a mathematical operation whereby the numerator
spies on the denominator
across the line of consciousness.

2.

When her firstborn was born,
she felt capable of exponential embrace—
of him, of her husband, of herself as mother.
She also felt twice as removed from the woman she was.
I'm taking off my thirties, she announced a few months later,
to a friend who didn't yet have children
and so couldn't know.
Yet it didn't seem like a caving in,
exactly—more like an essence dissolved in water.

3.

The decade was a tightrope
strung across a chasm.
Out of that chasm she heard echoes
and at its bottom she saw a stream.
Outcroppings of desperation
were smoothed by its current,
brooking no doubt.
Images played across the walls
like an outdoor movie. Her favorite
starred her two sons, lying on their stomachs,
propped on their elbows reading,

their upside-down legs waving absently
like the masts of moored sailboats
nudged by waves.

4.
The zeroes of 30 and 40
became lenses through which she glimpsed
lost cities in need of excavation.
She found a frieze
depicting her empty house
when she was alone in it.
She found frescoes illustrating
her family in stylized form
out walking by the canal in autumn
or a summer afternoon at the lake:
the blue rendered there
was the sky dipped in the sea, intensified.

5.
At 39 she weighed
the alternatives—to renew the lease
on disappearance
(to extend like an absence
so as to encompass riches)
or to send up flares.

How the Invisible Woman Sees Herself

Working alone in the house,
I look to the solitary sculls
passing on the river
for a sense that I am
among others.
The geese (my dogs)
convene in the yard
near the water.
A summer
in which much has passed
is now folded and put away.
The quiet is like a pie
behind glass, uncut.

The Invisible Woman Stands Out

I wait in the yard
on the hard ground,
outside my door on the river,
the air's foundling,
as though the earth
were meeting me
halfway through space.
The house is a vessel
stowing my family
safely out of sight
of time, while blue jays toss
in the clouds' foam.
As dusk materializes,
lamps break the code
of every other house.
The sky seems
as much my home.

III. A Procession of Fields

The Chosen Guide

"... and should the chosen guide
Be nothing better than a wandering cloud,
I cannot miss my way."
—Wordsworth

1

In the felled garden,
three last blossoms
of ground ivy, hooded,
purple, warded off the frost
with the armor of their color,
the aroma of their leaves
furring the cold.
One final harebell,
its death knell long since
sounded and unheeded,
its fellows evaporated
into heaven's summer fields,
laid its head upon stone.
At the feeders, among black-capped
chickadees and slate juncos,
a cardinal and blue jays
flipped a page

2

in this month's catalogue
of last colors.
November had always seemed
the bookmark of the year.
You'd leave off in October
to fix a cup of tea, the heroine
dying in a trail of love,
and resume in the swan-white spectacle
of loose ends tied up like

frozen currents. I was still dreamy,
October-headed; my eyes
projected memories of sugar-maple
hillsides sweetening the slide
to what I'd always seen as
only gray, as if redressing with rhymes

3
verse contentedly blank.
Gray: halfway house
of winter, the color
of water in a glass in an unlit room
at dusk, of whispers, fur
at the root, the shade
of shade, the cast of roads.
I turned from the house, crossed
the road into the sloping meadow,
and climbed with my heart
wide open to the sinking hills.
Wind-emptied trees
proclaimed a heyday
for evergreens. The feather-flowers
September's goldenrod had become
dressed me

4
in white initiation.
Then the woods took me in—
and my feet threshed
society's former beauties,
and my eyes cashed in
the beeches' late-minted
copper, and the tuning forks
of bare birches
rhymed my stride.

On this afternoon of clouds stalled
like posted letters waiting out
a national holiday,
I stalked exhilaration
like a bounty hunter,
half-hoping the wound
would be mine,
that through an opening
like the cleft in the old apple tree,
which wanted too badly
to lean all ways,
I'd be hounded

5
out of myself into a story
my footsteps would write.
From the clearing on the hilltop,
I saw shadows turn in
for the night. The sun
arrived opposite me
as at an opulent table.
And the wind, prompting
in the trees, helped me
find my place.

Postscript: The Harebell

The harebell, on her lissome,
now stooping stem, goes on and on
into the weather of snow
and lonely evergreens.
She presides over the frozen garden,
an orphan in the only house
her colors know.

I hear her sing
of an earthly everlastingness—
a woman's chivalry
toward all she loves.
To her my dreams go begging . . .
as if to wrestle free
of what they know is in store for me.

In November

1.
November is a gray ocean
into which the river of color empties.
At the mouth of the river
an indifferent god
accepts the sacrifice of warmth
culled from a pyre of leaves and twigs.
Smoke and cold currents
together stream away.

2.
I have moved to a house by the river
and find that the river
makes certain demands:
a concentration equal to its own.
Sitting by the bank,
I want to send the stray dogs
Impatience and Distraction
home to where they came from.

3.
Since summer I have been vigilant.
In August the property was one place,
and in November it is another.
I can tell you no tree was first,
and none was last.
I thought I would mourn
the sunlit green enclosures.
Now I relish the restoration
of the monarchy of clear sight,
with glints of silver,
shiverings of white.

4.

When the trees undress,
the view is unveiled
like a reclining nude.
In the cut-granite air,
I see the light's ancestral lines.
At sunset, I face the burning leaves
of the western sky, then turn
to the east's paler version.

5.

November is the god of self-scrutiny.
O November, don't mock
the illusions born of summer's azure.
See how the copper beech,
like a nervous mother,
still clutches her fluttering children.
On the sky's colorless shifting walls
see a memo of my life,
a *to*, a *from*, a *subject*,
and teach me to read
what follows.

East Hill Road

The mourning dove in the apple tree
meets the solitary apple that refused
to fall. The tree's last patients,
they commiserate in the empty blue.
Snow patches the dun path, a crumb-trail
of cold. By the pond two cattails,
having missed their cue to burst,
now stand helpless as Popsicles.
In love there is no such thing as choice,
but unlimited supplies of regret.
There, in your citrus-circled house,
on your canyon perch, the need for me
subsides like heat at evening.
Here, a whitening aisle
through a field, a river
parted from its current.

Brilliant

First Thought
The leaves are in their retirement. For some, it's the best
time of life: a free fall, or free-for-all, having paid one's dues
and—albeit less than cordially—shaken hands
with mortality. And what a show, the leaves' late coloratura!

Second Thought
By the mill in Broadalbin, at the pond's ardent request,
leaves step into the role of autumn water lilies, adrift in twos
and threes on lily pads of cloud. A crowd of evergreens stands
in the first ring, not leaving. Nor do I, the reviewer.

Autumn Suite

i.
Arrivals

We drove that September afternoon
under jigsaw clouds never quite
coming together, the sunlight a gel
of quelled heat, sunflowers burning out
along the road. Asters in their prime tolled
the death knell of black-eyed Susans.
Going nowhere, we arrived every second,
keeping pace with a procession of fields.
The less we said, the more I felt our personalities
expand. It was what we wanted, then—
no explanations, nothing checked off.

ii.
Pas de *Fall*

In October neurotic maples
excel, exquisitely attuned

to weather. Fraying color,
screaming color, weeping color,

till color slips away.
In the ensuing calm

the courtly evergreens
go on—old friends

with secrets left to tell.

iii.
Pastorale

November—adorning
the trees in their own
nakedness, fastening
the air with cold.
Do you remember?
I read the scrambled code
of your beauty. Claim me,
again, when dusk
flecks the river with geese.
The sky is soon
demolished. Life asks
to be let out.

Winter Aubade

How not to interrupt the morning's glistening
with the tread of thoughts? Goldfinches
patrol the feeder in their winter olive. Yet again
I fall back on them for signs of life, the finches
and the squirrels, who've made off with the apples
I tossed into the snow. Nothing approaches
the solitude of the oak. Great, occasional
thuds and crashes when snow and icicles
lose their grip on the roof. I often find myself
viewing the outer trappings of everyday life,
as though hovering just above our house:
a sense of place I calculate to infinity
streaming off from the decimal point of our bed.
Questions harvesting an answer.
If there is some other sensible place to be,
let it reveal itself like a ruin of the future.
Let me walk to it, picking my way along crumbling ice.
How not to wander from the path?
How not to interrupt the tread of thoughts
with distractions of the morning's glistening?

Snow Record

Stop, friend, and take a second view—
This dust here was once belov'd like you.
> —Gravestone inscription,
> New Hampshire churchyard

It's good that the sun rises:
that was the straight-faced thought
I had when I got up this morning
and saw the ragged semicircle
swell up from the woods
and make of the hall window
a picture frame for ticking time.

The snow is profoundly deep,
and the air deeply cold,
and sleep comes hard
toward the end of winter,
when I think of the deaths
I'm supposed to have grown used to.
Memory burns up upon entry.

First one downstairs, alone
in the still-sleeping kitchen,
I watch the shadow of a crow
cross the yard, a charcoal line
that erases as it goes. It's good
that earthworms lie in wait under snow,
among the undecided flowers.

Wolf

I caught the wolf
and carried it like a lamb,
my arms around its legs,
its body a raft of fur
under my chin.
It didn't struggle,
and my confidence didn't flag
as I walked down the block.
When the door opened
I slipped the wolf through,
sensing the excitement
of the small crowd inside.
I could see a woman
lighting wooden matches,
one after the other,
much too close to the face
of another woman,
whose eyelashes
were getting singed.
I stood on the corner,
the streets veering off
toward somewhere.
It was my wolf.
It was my wolf.

'February, and the low-lying vistas'

February, and the low-lying vistas
failed to transport,
like a train that missed us.
The wind made short
work of knowing the trees:
we longed for negotiations
of leaf and breeze.
Flowerbeds languished like abandoned stations.
Even the deer—standing still,
calmly feeding—
deprived us of the thrill
of strangers meeting.

The Closed Forest

In memory of Joseph L. Weininger

Into the closed forest he went, with no
shirt, no watch, no wallet. Something
arranged it so that we weren't allowed
to watch him make the necessary gesture,
or ever know exactly how the space
that has no opening and no close was opened
and closed. And nothing was traded
for him—now there is only none
of him and more of the same. When we gathered,
one star for each of us briefly
wrung itself in the heavens, and then
was through. Through to something he went,
given roots for next of kin and earth
for earth, and no things except the spaces
between them. The shovel was handed round.
The rain brought altitudes down to him.
The globe seemed to shrink, what with our
demand for it to hold this gift.
Nothing was traded for him in the closed forest.

IV. Stars or Other Distances

First Day at San Ramón

In memory of Thelma de Vera

By the front door of San Ramón,
far below the equator,
I sit in a wicker chair
and the *tacuarita* sings,
little brown bird erasing
the portrait of a reluctant traveler,
and I pledge allegiance
to my newfound Fred Astaire
who makes me the heir
to his happiness, here
in the arbor of wisteria
not yet in bloom.
All through the morning
I have been watching
the short white horse
tied to the fence
near the red nasturtiums.
He calls out across the fields
for proof he is not the last
horse on earth.
No answer but from the sheep
grazing around Halley House,
their bleating an audible shimmer.
A layer of sound
over the deeper layer
of silence. Thoughts
seem too loud,
too human. A rebellion
ignited by blossoms,
the gold bristling puffs
that seem to explode
from the *espinillo*,

gnarled tree of the pastures,
which Lolo tells me is good for nothing
save the saintly scent
of its flowers. South, I see,
is no mirror of the north,
and I revel
in having no reflection.

—*Entre Ríos, Argentina*

Alplaus After Argentina

The late-turning sugar maple
talks back to me, determined
to have the last word
on beauty. But memories of San Ramón
keep crossing the borders
of consciousness to stay.
There, time lumbered harmlessly
as in a holding tank.
All through the afternoons
while the rest of the family went riding,
I sat with my books on the stone terrace,
turning my chair toward the sun,
as placid as the cattle in the fields.
The *loros*, the wild parrots, turned the silence
inside out as they sampled the tops
of the eucalyptus trees, then
shook it out again as they
flashed green across the sky.
And I remember
the soaring *carancho*'s
white underwing;
the sawgrass ceilings
sloping above us as my beloved
delved into sleep;
and Bernardo the white horse,
waiting in the rose of sunrise.

Long Distance

At the gas station on La Brea,
I felt an easterner's awe
at the purple aura of the jacarandas.
We'd spent the afternoon
driving around, stopping for coffee
and old books, talking and not talking,
you with that lifelong look in your eyes
of stunned resignation.

Snow falling here now. Dusk
wraps around the spruces
in their white dresses.
I keep the lights off
so I can watch the falling,
and seem to see the tracks
of our history covered over,
word-ghosts of conversations.

It's the countless amnesias,
you like to say, that keep handing us our lives.

Birdwatching in Malibu

At the freshwater lagoon in Malibu,
our first find was the great blue heron,
which seemed to incise the afternoon
air. Your Nikon clicks skittered

across the coots' Marx Brothers chatter.
But the great blue was outdone
by the common egret, white
as a shell, posed like a question

mark, philosopher of still water.
Grebes and their young reminded us
of cartoons. Life imitates all the things
we know from our experience of life.

As we continued on the path to the beach,
fish jumped clear into the air,
their silver bodies like momentary ornaments
strung on our line of sight, or like flashes

of insight. And then the sea, saying
drumroll, please, and then *never mind,
this might take a while*. Gulls
lolled on the strip of sand dividing

sea from lagoon, but plovers
plighted their troth to the constantly shifting
edge of froth. A willet, like a pen in ink,
dipped its long thin bill between

glistening stones. The sun
was dropping now. Cormorants, like outdoor
concertgoers who leave before the encore
and stream toward the parking lots,

flew across the lagoon to a eucalyptus
on the other side of the coast highway.
We watched them assemble there
before taking one last detour

to find the yellow-headed blackbirds,
heard but not seen in an edifice of reeds.
A man who'd been playing guitar
to the indifferent water packed up

for the night. Serene, he seemed to have
seized his day. We accepted
that some of the birds we saw
will remain nameless. We got back

in the car, and the lanes of traffic
on the highway were somehow welcoming
as they absorbed us. Everyone
was trying to get somewhere,

and this seemed to make sense,
while the Pacific alongside us
stayed put, sure of itself, not
needing us, or dinner, or love.

A Birthday Poem

Here is where
the barred owl
called to me,
and I called you,
and held the phone
up toward high branches
in my eastern dusk,
your LA afternoon,
so you could hear
the almost comic truth
of the common rendering
of this bird's call in English—
Who cooks for you?
Who cooks for you?—
and so you could know,
as in earlier days
when we shared Manhattan
like a soda with two straws,
what yet another random hour
of my life is like.
(Your consciousness
is the mirror
without which I'd be
invisible to myself.)
This time it's a flock of sparrows
on branches ripe with snow,
horses in the field
barely moving
but for their breath
patching the February air,
and a woodpecker
in the hemlocks,
the reliable hemlocks
resisting change
along the roadside.

Other Distances

A perfect candidate for Miss
Morbidity, I often wake
at 4 a.m. to hear the hiss
of life evaporating from the lake

of itself. The cat, a charcoal smudge
on blue pillows, smothers me in fur.
Blind and deeply in need of touch,
he meets my terror

inch for inch. I never go downstairs
to watch TV or have a snack.
I lie still, trying not to think of stars
or other distances, the track

of years and the level crossing,
only my blood turning and tossing.

A Wedding Poem

As the horizon marries land to sky,
Limning infinities of finite days,
In this man and this woman
Sacred oneness displays
A new resplendence.
Roses approach *you* for
Advice on beauty. Travelers, you
Find your place in each other's
Ardor, making circles out of lines.
Evening rises in the sunken garden, and
Love encloses time.

In Memory of the New York Times

Don't ask me, said the daylily to the bee—
the flower unfolding in the morning air
like a newspaper, the bee diving in
like my father, his forehead above the headlines
the beacon of my childhood.
So well-loved, so well-tended!—a blossom
of many petals, and a fresh one every day,
crowning the kitchen table with its glorious
indifference. Reading was punctuated
by quick surveys of the yard (to which, like all
good Americans, he was devoted): its daily weather,
its stars of lilac or late phlox and stripes
of mown rows of grass, the million fallen
idols of sugar maples or the birdless new snows.
Early on I learned that nature's
destined companion is print.
I asked nothing but received perfect answers,
replied the bee, on its way.

My Father's Copy of Herzog

On the couch under lamplight,
my father reading, his head propped on a sunken
pillow, at the far end of the living room
between the picture window and the fireplace,
opposite my mother's reading chair
and the matching chair the cat reserved
for himself: this was the first holy space I knew.
Ashes mounting in the ashtray on the coffee table
like a pile of raked leaves.

I'm a throwback every time I lie down to read in the evenings,
or go out in my yard with a rake or shovel.
The puzzle of the genes: is there one
for loving reading, or looking after a bit of land?
His library, forced off of shelves by my own,
fills my attic. Out of the mountains of history
and politics I keep the novels in separate boxes,
and just last week picked up *Herzog*. Blue cloth cover,
jacketless, spine lit up in silver letters.

In the pages I find a slip of paper that I'm sure
will be something he'd jotted down while reading,
a direct link to his mind, whose company
I'd barely had the pleasure of, the whole thing
being over when I was sixteen. Just a torn piece
of the lost jacket, perhaps his bookmark.

Instead of faith, I have the sensation
of my fingertips' turning the same pages his turned.
Instead of faithlessness, I have the sense that the self
is so sculpted by—dented by—experience
as to obliterate the pure and constant thing
a man or woman for a lifetime tries to know.
"And as for his relation to the dead,

it was very bad indeed. He really believed
in letting the dead bury their own dead.
And that life was life only
when it was understood clearly as dying."

The crispness of the corner of a page grasped
between thumb and forefinger,
the whisper of its turning like dry leaves swept
upward, like breath inhaled.

Consolations of the Kitchen Table

1.
Frank Sinatra was singing "My Way"
on TV. I was six or seven.
I had recently learned the meaning
of *yahrzeit* candles and had decided
that I, for one, was going to live forever.
Midway through the song
I went to my mother, sitting
at the kitchen table,
and told her I had a stomachache.
I put my head in her lap.
As it strikes me now,
I put my life in her life.

2.
"I have been thinking a *lot*
about what it feels like to be dead,"
my eight-year-old tells me,
his eyes and forehead scrunched
as though squinting against the sun.
He takes a bit of my hair
between his fingers, as he has done
ever since his mint-green baby blanket
shredded like a cloud.
What would comfort him,
now that he's growing up out of the safe house
of the present tense?
I say something about the soul,
but it's no match for a boy's image of bones.
Unconsoled, he goes on, bracing himself
for the sound of his fears:
"You're 41, you don't have much longer to live.

And I don't want you to die."
He hugs me, he puts his life in my life.
Like two survivors embracing
we look over each other's shoulders
to where neither of us is.

Two Anecdotes for Mothers

1.

"Is it round like the Earth?" Ethan asked
when I told him I had a lollipop
stashed in my purse. Flash
to a four-year-old's assortment
of ways to be round . . .
"Actually, it's round like a penny," I replied.
A sigh of disappointment, but it would do.
And a flicker of approval—that my mind's eye
had winked at his.

2.

"Did she pop?" Zachary, then three,
asked about my mother.
It took me a few moments,
and then I saw his theory.
His grandmother, coveted in memory,
had vanished like a balloon.
I think I said something like yes.
Two years later, again on the subject
of her and dying, he went diving
under the table as though for cover—
finding no haven (too much like me)
in the idea of heaven.

Grade Crossing

A long, slow freight train at the grade crossing
is sometimes a welcome sight.
Alone and in no hurry,
you can cease to be the driver
of your own fate. You keep your hands
on the wheel, but the steering
is of thoughts, or the rush of air
through the dry streambed
where thoughts are meant to run.
Meanwhile other drivers make U-turns,
subtracting their dot from the line,
and might in fact beat you
by taking the long way around.
You sit, happy in your state of suspension,
until the train trails off
like a sentence with no end punctuation,
like experience being threaded through
to the past. You've been aware
that your face was visible
to the driver of the car ahead,
reflected in his rearview mirror.
You can't completely dream
unless you are alone at the grade crossing,
or first in line—otherwise
you keep the mask of waiting on,
the way a child, writing something
private, or possibly incorrect,
curves her hand around
the edge of the page
like a fence, or a shield.

Gratitude

Learn to be grateful for armchairs, where you fit
  like a nut in its shell. Consider that plum blossoms
happen twice: once in the vase, once as shadow.
  And these double windows and quadruple doors—
all have been constructed to slow the passage
  of air, feet, time. You come through
in the morning and by afternoon, the day is
    something: a shadow's inches, a stanza, an emptied coffee cup.

And things have their correspondences:
  Cézanne's boy always walks toward you
like the future. The chairs' foreheads
  gentle the clamor of unobserved cells in a room—
as the face of your beloved
  answers for all of you.

Between the eye and its sighted object
  a chronicle of personality takes place.
All you need to know about me
  is that I love the piled-on rectangles of a room,
the window admitting the hill's diagonal,
  birches' white strokes on a green band.
Near-sighted eyes arrange the page
  at a slant, which the heart interprets as stairs.

Acknowledgments

Thanks to the editors of the following publications, where poems in this book, some in slightly different versions, first appeared.

Agni: "First Day at San Ramón"
The Atlantic: "The Invisible Woman," "The Closed Forest," "Gratitude"
The Nation: "East Hill Road"
National Review: "How the Invisible Woman Sees Herself" (under the title "Among Others"), "Pleasant Bay," "Part of a Lifetime"
The New Criterion: "Brilliant"
The New Republic: "At Steepletop"
Poetry: "A Hundred Skies" (under the title "Native"), "Sightseeing with the Invisible Woman," "The Invisible Woman Continued," "Snow Record"
Poetry Ireland Review: "The Chosen Guide"
The Republic of Letters: "To R., on His Ocean Adventure"
Salmagundi: "In Memory of the *New York Times*"
Southern Review: "Postscript: The Harebell," "The Invisible Woman Surfaces," "My Father's Copy of *Herzog*," "The White Pines"
Southwest Review: "The Less I See"
The Times Literary Supplement: "February, and the low-lying vistas"
Verse: "Second Day on Garnet Lake," "Third Day on Garnet Lake"
Yale Review: "Cold Comfort"
Yankee: "Song for Five O'Clock"

Thanks also to the Millay Colony for the Arts for two residencies during which several poems in this book were written.

The song cycle *Three Poems of Jessica Hornik,* a setting by Joseph Hallman of "Pleasant Bay," "Postscript: The Harebell," and "East Hill Road," was recorded by Inscape Chamber Orchestra (Sono Luminus). The suite of poems *Raving Beauty,* also a song cycle by Hallman, was commissioned by, and first performed at, the Rosenbach Museum in Philadelphia.

CPSIA information can be obtained
at www.ICGtesting.com
Printed in the USA
FFHW021820041118
49212130-53448FF